STRESS MANAGEMENT
Workplace Wellness Ideas That Only Take Minutes To Do To Avoid Work Burnout and Reduce Anxiety and Stress.

YOU WILL LEARN TO FOCUS THE MIND, ENERGIZE THE BODY, BE ALERT, CALM, AND MANAGE STRESS.

This book introduces you to practical stress reducing activities, to start, finish, and manage your day.

Library and Archives Canada Cataloguing in Publication

Mackie, Paul, 1951 - author
Stress Management - Paul Mackie.

ISBN: 978-1-988986-44-9 (softcover)

Copyright© 2024 by Paul Mackie
All rights reserved. No part of this book may be reproduced, or utilized in any form, or by any means, electronic, mechanical or photocopying (unless stated in this book), without permission in writing from the Author.

Contents

ABOUT THIS BOOK AND THE AUTHOR

Hi, Paul Mackie here, at the age of 27 I looked like I was 50 years old, the worst part was, I felt like I was 50 years old; now at the age of 72 I feel better than I did when I was 27.

At 27 years old I smoked 40 cigarettes a day and socially drank alcohol on my lunch break at the local pub.

Realizing that at 27 years old I looked twice my age; and nearly blinding my supervisor in a work accident, I decided to stop smoking and drinking; this book will show you how I did that; and learned to manage daily stress:

You Will Learn:

- Use easy to do movements to manage in the moment stress.
- Avoid workplace burnout.
- How I Stopped smoking and drinking.
- How I Reversed my aging process.
- 5 ways to meditate.
- Use balance to clear excessive thoughts and focus the mind.
- How to use more of your Brain's potential.
- A 5-minute exercise to start and finish your day.

Everything in this book has been used by the author to get through and manage his day in some stressful and dangerous work environments.

The author also realized that apart from the activities presented in this book, there is one vital thing that must be done to stop workplace burnout and mental breakdowns; the author shows you how.

In the early stages of my work career, I used to drink alcohol, and smoke 40 cigarettes a day, which helped me deal with the stress of a fast paced and dangerous work environment. Every workday was a struggle, and no matter how hard I tried, I could not stop the chatter in my mind.

Today using certain activities, I do not drink, or smoke; and feel a lot healthier in my 70's than I did in my 20's; my mind is focused in the moment and is clear of excessive chatter; here is how I did that:

- A 5-minute exercise to start your day.
- How to focus in the moment.
- Use more of your brain's potential.
- How to be energized and feel youthful.
- How to reduce anxiety and stress.
- Be motivated to start and explore every workday.

This book explains how to do each activity, and gives a visual, printable picture page, to help guide you when using the activities.

Consistency is the key, when using the movements.

Over the years, I learned ways to cope with life's challenges; to take those leaps of faith out of the box and explore my full potential; to walk a balanced purposeful life.

Motivational Movements are the start to your day, along with the other motivational activities in this book; to make every day a meaningful day.

I present the motivational activities in the hope that they work for you, as they have for me and others in my care.

Remember this:
- "Don't look back," you're not going that way.
- No matter how you feel, get up, dress up, show up, and never give up.
- You don't always have to be right.
- Live in the moment, it is all we have.
- Do the 5-minute exercise shown in this book twice a day.

DISCLAIMER: The stress management activities provided in this book are intended for educational and informational purposes only. The author is not a licensed therapist or healthcare professional, and the activities should not be considered a substitute for professional advice, diagnosis, or treatment. Readers should consult with a qualified healthcare provider or therapist before implementing any stress management techniques, especially if they have pre-existing medical conditions or concerns.

The author and publisher disclaim any liability arising from the use or misuse of the information provided in this book.

AVOIDING BURN OUT - IT IS VITAL THAT YOU:

- **MAKE TIME FOR YOURSELF.**
- **DO SOMETHING CREATIVE FOR YOURSELF.**
- **USE THIS BOOK'S 5 MINUTE EXERCISE TWICE DAILY.**

SOME ACTIVITIES TO HELP BEAT STRESS ARE:

- Breathing
- Balance board
- Energizing the body
- Meditation
- Motivational movements
- Relaxation activities
- Sensory environment
- Have a clear workspace
- Visualization
- Personal creative time (very important)
- Handy brain movements.

A 5-MINUTE EXERCISE TO START YOUR DAY
Watch On Youtube.com: https://youtu.be/av7FOZNb_Vc

WHAT A BREAKDOWN LOOKS LIKE

At the age of 50 I had a break down; you're probably wondering how that could happen knowing all the stress management techniques that I knew?

At the time of my breakdown, I was working with people who had disabilities; I had my own team working with the toughest clients, the ones no one wanted; mainly because of severe behavior issues.

I worked with these clients for 5 years, then one day it hit me like a ton of bricks; I had a breakdown.

The day was like any other, I headed off to work on the local train service; I got on the train, sat down and then a weird thing happened; it felt like I could hear everything.

The noise level increased to the point where it was deafening; then it felt like everyone on the crowded train was pushing in on me; I got off at the next stop and walked home.

The next day the same thing happened; I decided to go and visit a counsellor.

The counsellor quickly got to the bottom of the problem, telling me I was burned out and having anxiety attacks, but that was not the problem.

I paid two visits to the counsellor and realised that my job had kept me so busy that I had stopped meditating; stopped my creative activities, no sports or exercising; my job had consumed me.

It took six weeks off work to get back to a point where I could go on the train and go to work; but I had changed.

I was meditating, writing books, doing my 5-minute exercises, and doing more creative things for myself; I decided to re-evaluate my life; I changed careers again and became an Apartment Building Manager.

While being an Apartment Building manager was somewhat stressful, doing my exercises, leaving my work at work, and finding time for myself and family kept me feeling good about life until I retired.

P.S: Don't be afraid to seek professional help; I thought I was a very strong person, both mentally and physically; but I was wrong.

STRESS MANAGEMENT MOVEMENTS

POSSIBILITIES:
- Clear thinking.
- Increased energy and relaxation.
- Accessing both sides of the brain for creative thinking.
- How to focus on and solve problems.
- Increased energy.
- Increased listening skills.
- Feeling motivated.
- Start your day off in a positive way.

Stress Management Movements are best done standing, but most can be done sitting or lying down.

Stress Management Movements should be done as soon as you wake up or get out of bed.

Stress Management Movements can be done individually for an energy boost, or to help calm, relax and bring balance to the mind and body.

It is the author's hope that the activities in this book will help you to balance mind, body, and spirit, so you can live an active, purposeful, and meaningful life.

Cautions and Disclaimer:

It is advisable to consult a doctor before using the activities in this book.

The suggested activities do not consider the age, cognitive ability, or any physical problems the participants in the activity may have.

Is said to help with: Oxygenating the brain.

Why it is useful: Water helps conduct the electrical and chemical processes of the brain for clear thinking; computer work; operating machinery; and organizational activities.

How it is done: Having a water bottle close by is an easy way to take a drink during the workday.

Is said to help with: Increased energy and relaxation.

Why it is useful: An energy boost when needed keeps you alert and energized during the workday; for paying attention to details; and filling out paperwork.

How it is done: Place your hand on your neck (palm on the Adam's apple) with thumb on one side and fingers on the other. Move your hand down until you feel your collarbone jump over it and massage the soft spots between the next set of ribs and the collarbone. Place your other hand on your belly button (do not massage with this hand).

Switch both hands and repeat for about 30 seconds.

Is said to help with: Accessing the whole brain.

Why it is useful: Using both sides of the brain are essential for reading; writing; creativity; comprehension; body coordination; public speaking; and stress reduction.

How it is done: Lift your left leg and touch your left knee with your right hand. Put the foot down and lift your right leg and touch your right knee with your left hand; repeat three or more times.

Participants having difficulty can match colored bands or stickers placed on opposite hands and knees.

Is said to help with: De-stressing and focusing on problems.

Why it is useful: Being relaxed and focused helps make your workday easier; improves self-esteem; leading meetings; seeing others' point of view; and multi-tasking.

How it is done: Stand up straight, or you can sit or lie on the floor, cross your feet at the ankles, and give yourself a big hug by placing your hands under each arm pit; can be done standing, sitting, or lying down.

Is said to help with: Listening, balance and memory.

Why it is useful: Developing the ability to listen, retain information; memory; and have whole body co-ordination are essential skills for good social interaction.

How it is done: Tilt your head, placing your ear on your shoulder, while extending your arm forward. With your hand draw an infinity sign (an 8 on its side) the width of your shoulders, focusing your eyes beyond the fingertips.

Your body and arm move as one unit with no twisting on the hips. Do several times with each arm.

Is said to help with: Energy and verbal expression.

Why it is useful: Having more energy; a relaxed jaw and facial muscles make it easier for you to communicate; public speaking; and handling objections.

How it is done: Put your fingers on your cheeks.

Find the pivotal points of the jaw by opening and closing the jaw.

While yawning, massage the points with your fingers.

A yawning or roaring sound can be made.

Is said to help with: Listening and focusing skills.

Why it is useful: Attention is taken away from other activities while helping you to focus and listen; answering telephones; following instructions; and speaking clearly.

How it is done: Grasp each ear with the thumb on the inside rim and the pointer finger on the outside rim; uncurl the ear down to the ear lobe using the pointer finger along with the thumb; bring pointer finger and thumb back to the top of the ear and repeat several times.

BALANCE BOARD

AN EXCEPTIONAL PIECE OF EQUIPMENT THAT HELPS TO FOCUS THE MIND AND BALANCE THE BODY.

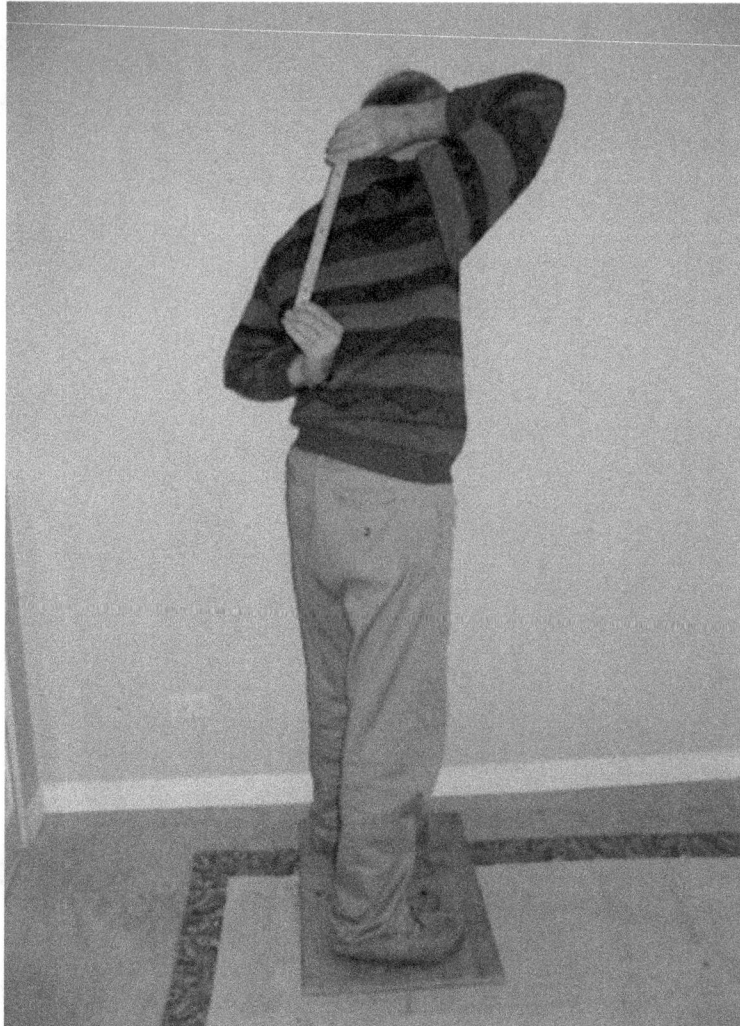

The stick should be 24 inches long; if you are more flexible a 16 or 12-inch stick can be used.

Pass the stick over your right shoulder with your right hand, grab the stick with your left hand as shown in the picture; then pass the stick with your left hand over your left shoulder and grab it with your right hand; alternate passing the stick over right and left shoulders.

Count aloud the number of passes in 1 minute.

Possible benefits: focusing the mind; reducing the mind's chatter and excessive thoughts; body coordination and concentration.

Note: The Balance Board adds another level of difficulty; passing Stick can be done without standing on the Balance Board.

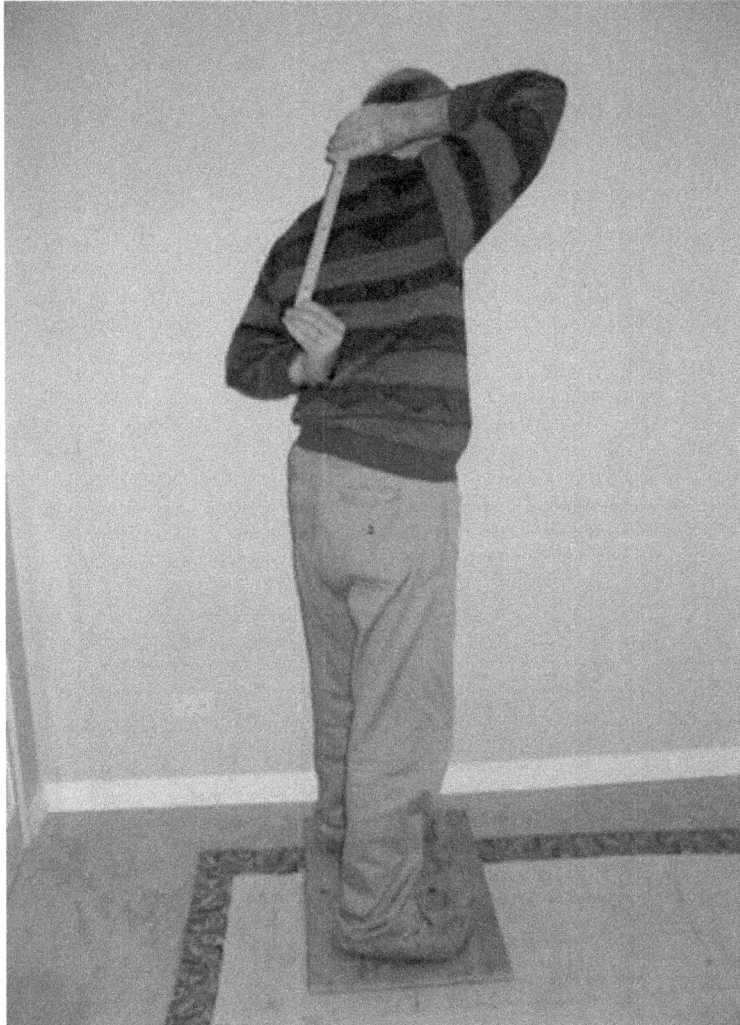

Pass the stick over your left shoulder, then your right shoulder.

Count to 100 in various numbers, then back to zero (Easy: 1, 5, 10s Harder: 3, 4, 7s).

Possible benefits: focusing the mind; body coordination and concentration; being able to figure out difficult tasks; number sequencing; increased memory.

The Adjustable Balance Board:
The board Is made from ¾ inch good one side plywood.

The boards optimal size is 24 inches x 16 inches (you will get 10 boards from a 4 foot x 8 foot sheet of plywood).

The board has adjustable rockers, to adjust the level of difficulty.

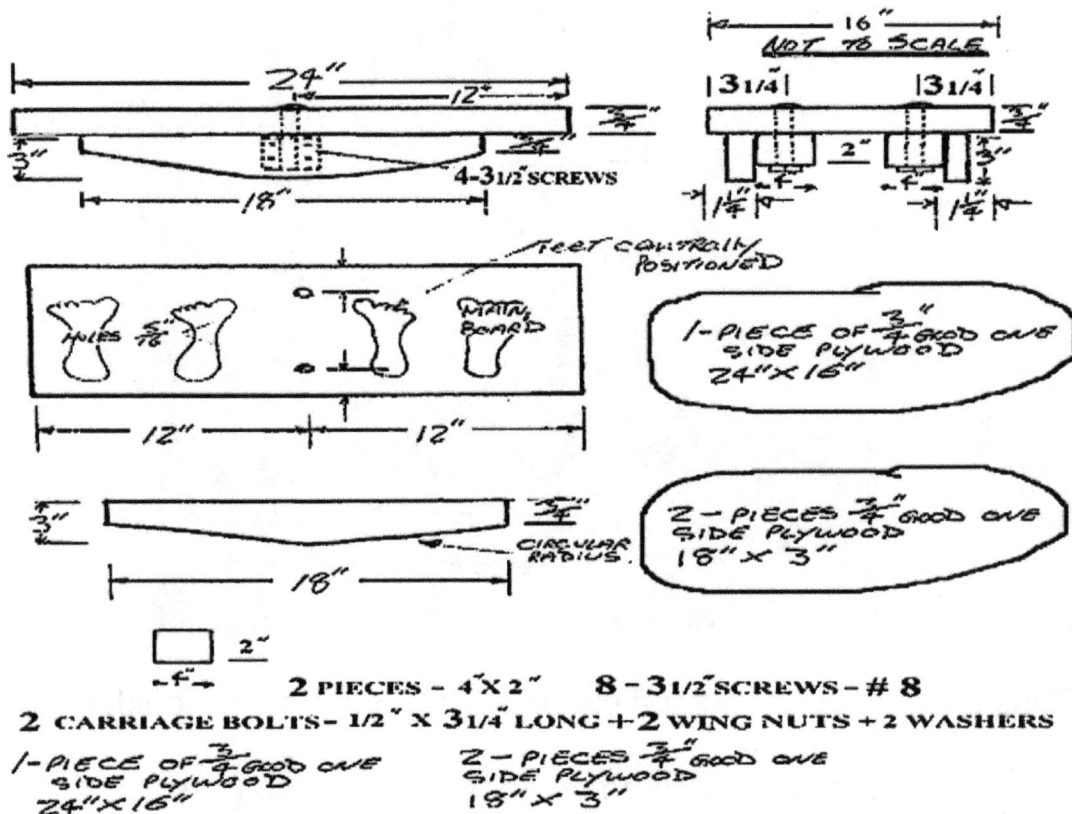

The Passing Stick
Made from a 1/2-inch piece of round Dowling, 24 inch or 12 inches (if you have more flexibility), rounded off at both ends.

You can take the sketch to a carpenter; or you can buy the Balance Board from Amazon, but it is not adjustable.

POSSIBILITIES
- Increased health.
- Feeling youthful.

I present each benefit and activity in this book as a possibility; keeping in mind, "What works for me may not work for you".

I suggest you try the movements and see how they work for you.

I firmly believe that these two movements helped reverse my feeling old and here's why:

At the age of 27 I looked like I was 50 years old, the worst part was, I felt like I was 50 years old; now at the age of 72 I feel better than I did when I was 27.

At 27 years old I smoked 40 cigarettes a day and socially drank alcohol on my lunch break at the local pub.

The company I worked for had a Christmas party, which I attended; the next day one of my coworkers showed me a picture of our team at the party.

My coworker pointed to a guy sitting at the table in the picture; he asked me, "Who is that?"

I replied, "That is me."

He replied, "No, that is not you, you are only 27, that guy is an old man and must be at least 50".

The problem was I felt like I was 50 years old, and I was the guy in the picture; that was the day I decided to change my life.

I told another coworker about the picture and told him that I needed to stop smoking 40 cigarettes a day and to stop drinking; he suggested I learn to meditate.

A couple of weeks later I learned Transcendental Meditation, which was the first step in my transformation.

The next step was to stop smoking; that was one of the hardest things I have ever had to do in my life.

But, before I tell you how I stopped smoking and drinking, let us look at the two Chi Kung movements that I believe reversed my state of health and how I felt about my age.

At 72, people tell me I look younger, but the reality is, it is not about how you look, it is about how you feel.

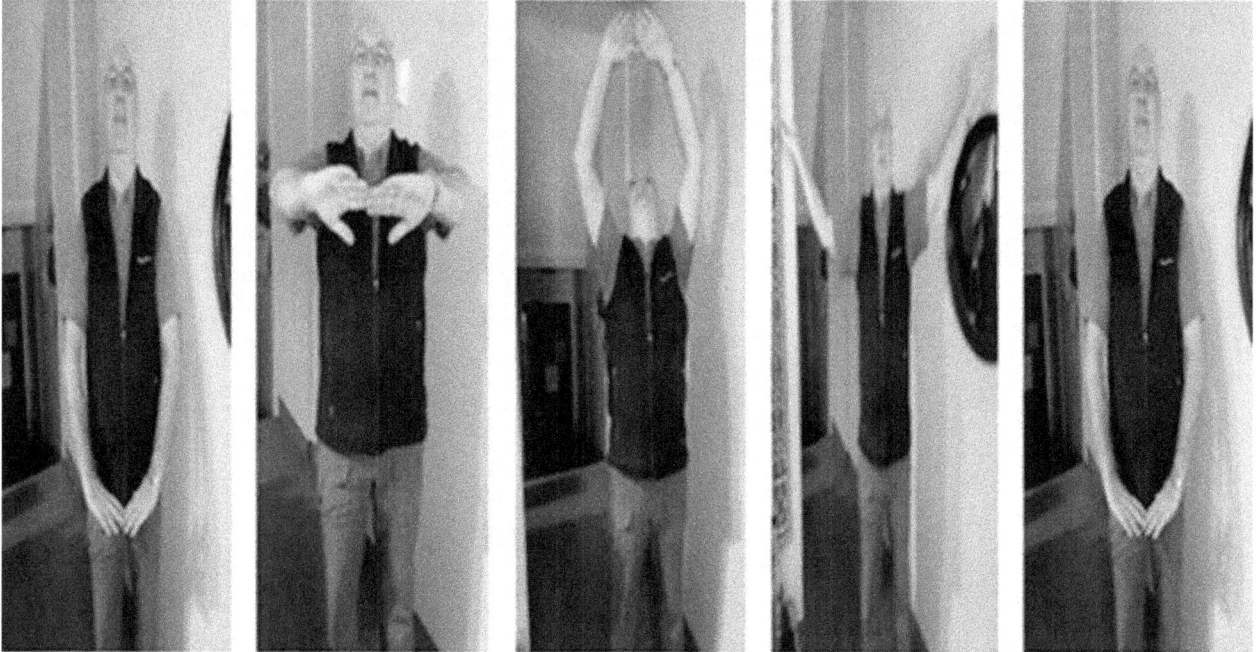

POSSIBILITIES

- Increased health.
- Increased focus and clearing the mind.

Stand relaxed with your knees slightly bent, arms down, and fingers pointing in towards each other.

Breathe in, through your nose as you push your arms forward and upwards, push palms up, still at right angles towards the ceiling.

Hold your breath as you look up.

Lower your arms down to your sides as you gently breathe out and lower your head (repeat 3 times).

NOTE: If you are a beginner at this movement, just breathe naturally, anyway you like; over time you will notice and adapt your breathing.

Once you have mastered the basic movement technique, another added step is to visualize energy flowing into the body as you raise your palms up to the sky.

CARRYING THE MOON FOR YOUTHFULNESS

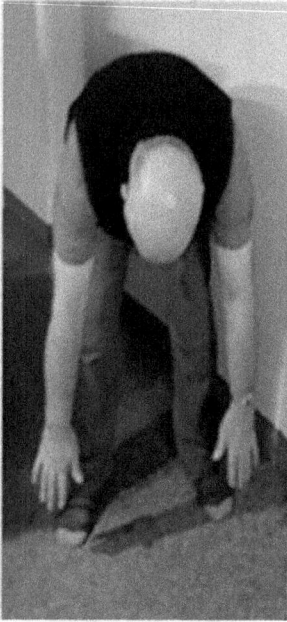

POSSIBILITIES

- Maintain youthfulness.
- Feel more relaxed.

Stand relaxed and upright, knees slightly bent.

Bend your body forward so that your arms hang down effortlessly in front.

Hold your breath, form a circle, with thumbs and index Fingers; straighten your body slowly, (breathe in through your nose) lifting your arms with the elbows straight in an arc to the front then above your head.

Continue backwards and slightly arch your back. hold your breath for a few seconds.

Visualize that you are in a shower of energy, flushing all negativity from your body, imagine the negative energy flowing out from your feet.

Straighten your body and lower your arms to the side as you breathe out, hold for a few seconds (repeat 3 times).

NOTE: If you are a beginner at this movement, just breathe naturally, anyway you like; over time you will notice and adapt your breathing.

Once you have mastered the basic movement technique, another added step is to visualize energy flowing into the body as you raise your palms up to the sky.

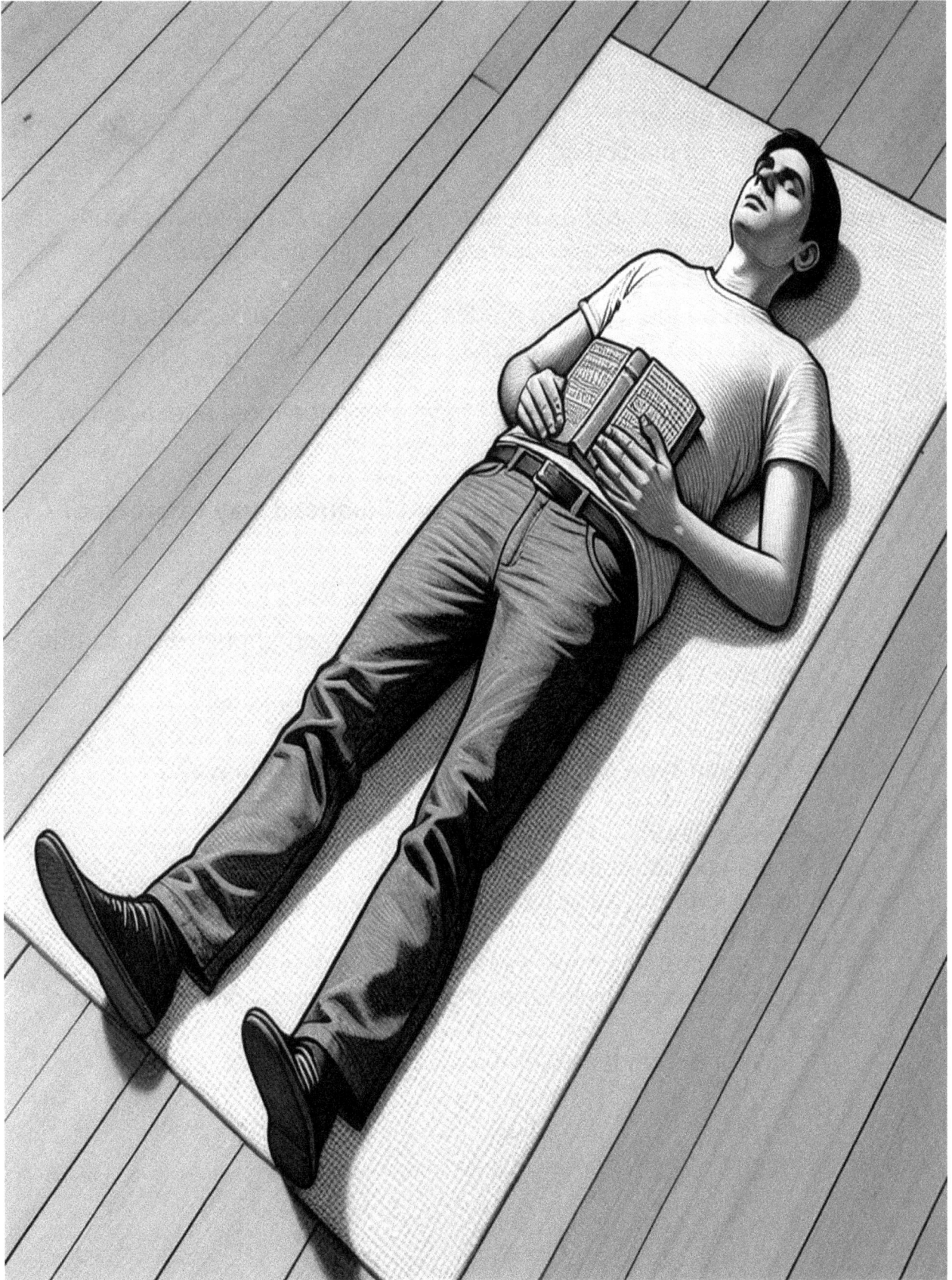

STOMACH BREATHING

POSSIBILITIES
- Focus the mind.
- Reduce stress.
- A focus for meditation.

Yes, as obvious as it sounds breathing is crucial to our survival but doing it correctly can help focus the mind and reduce stress.

Breathing can be the focus for meditation, relaxing, or focusing the attention to solve a problem you may be dealing with.

There are many ways to breathe; I have found the most effective way to breathe is from the stomach.

Purpose: To develop an energetic and balanced way to breathe.

1. Lie on the floor.
2. Place a book or object on your stomach.
3. Breathe in through the nose, your stomach should expand (the book should rise).
4. Breathe out through the mouth (the book should fall).

A more focused type of breathing can be done this way:

1. Lie on the floor.
2. Place a book or object on your stomach.
3. Breathe in through the nose, your stomach and then your chest should expand.
4. Hold your breath for as long as is comfortable.
5. Breathe out through the mouth your chest and stomach should fall.
6. Hold your breath for as long as is comfortable and repeat.

STOMACH BREATHING

Breath in through your nose, the stomach (book) should rise.

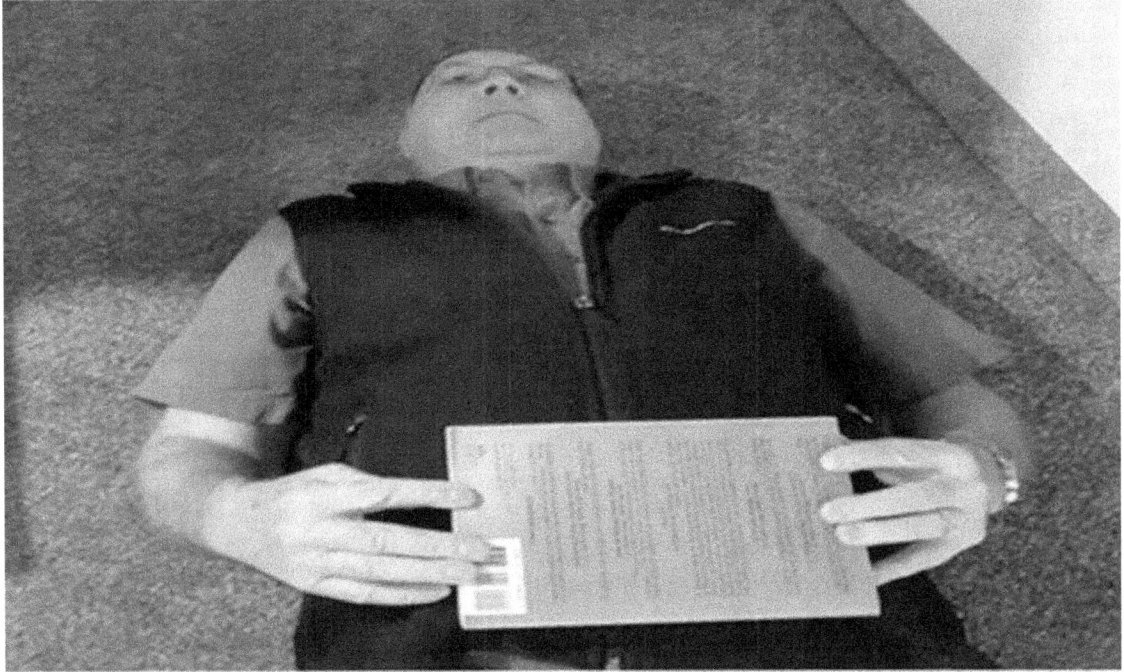

Breath out through your mouth, the stomach (book) should fall.

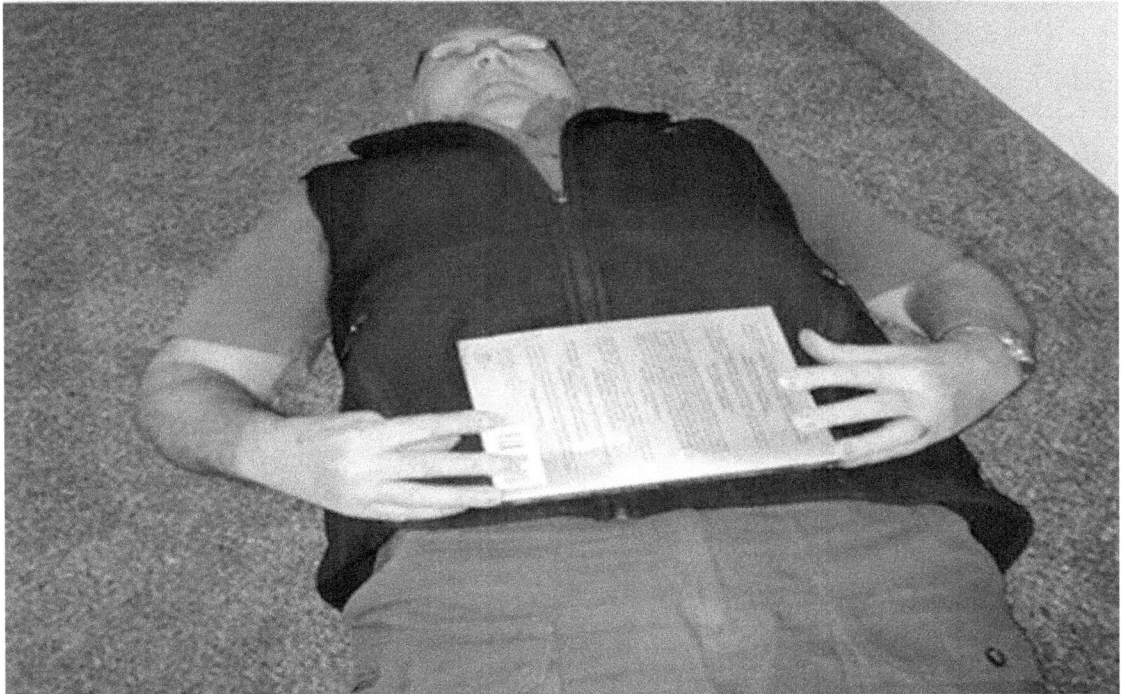

USING BOTH HANDS AT THE SAME TIME

USING MORE OF THE BRAIN'S POTENTIAL

Using both hands at the same time, also known as bilateral coordination, can support brain development and here's 7 reasons why:

1. **Enhanced Brain Connectivity:** Engaging both hands simultaneously promotes communication between the left and right hemispheres of the brain, fostering improved neural connectivity.
   Activity: Handy Brain Movements; coloring pictures with both hands.

2. **Improved Motor Skills:** Bilateral coordination activities help develop fine motor skills, such as handwriting, drawing, and manipulating objects, which are crucial for everyday tasks and academic success.
   Activity: Passing The Stick; Crossovers; Handy Brain Movements.

3. **Cognitive Development:** Tasks requiring bilateral coordination often involve problem-solving, spatial awareness, and visual-motor integration, contributing to overall cognitive development.
   Activity: Passing The Stick; Friendly Wave; Handy Brain Movements.

4. **Language Development:** Some bilateral activities, like clapping to a rhythm or playing musical instruments, can enhance auditory processing and language skills.
   Activity: Listening Ears: Handy Brain Movements; Massage Yawn.

5. **Emotional Regulation:** Bilateral activities can have a calming effect on the nervous system, promoting emotional regulation and stress reduction.
   Activity: Connections; Passing The Stick: Lifting The Sky.

6. **Social Interaction:** Many activities that involve using both hands simultaneously, such as playing team sports or collaborative art projects, encourage social interaction and cooperation.
   Activity: Carrying The Moon; Handy Brain Movements; Coloring.

7. **Cross-Lateral Movement:** Bilateral movements that cross the midline of the body stimulate both brain hemispheres and may facilitate learning and memory retention.
   Activity: Crossovers; Handy Brain Movements; Friendly Wave.

HANDY BRAIN MOVEMENTS – FLIP HANDS

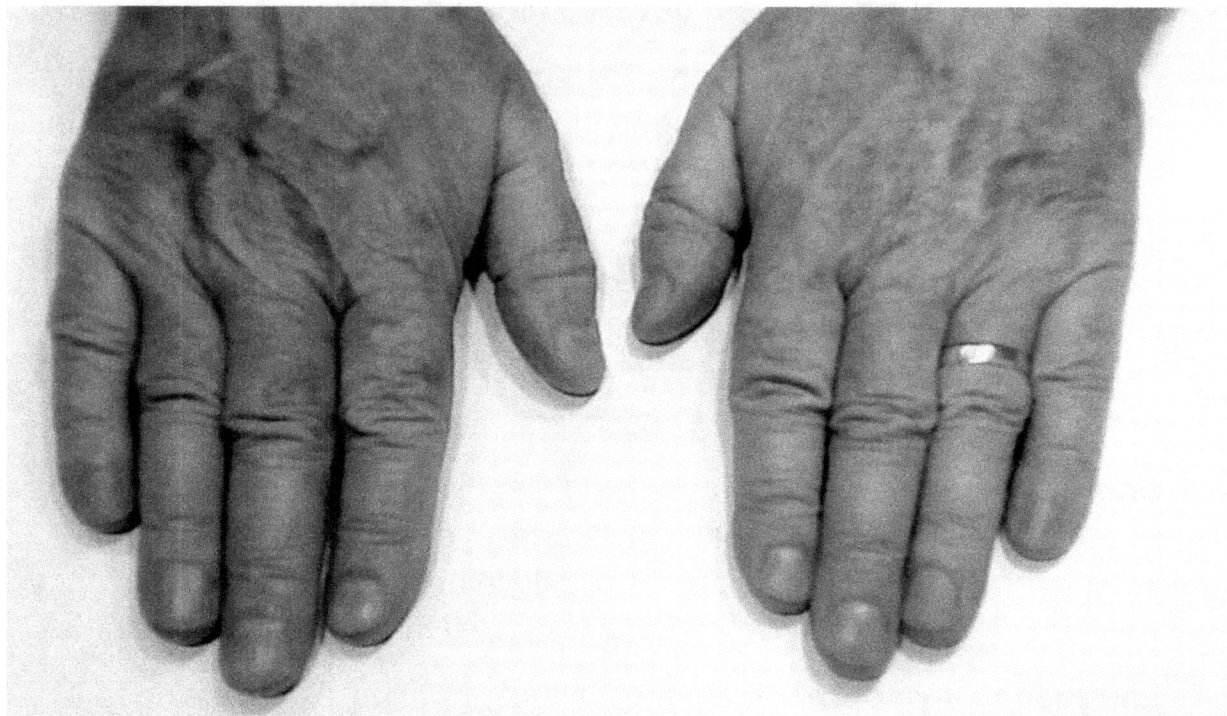

HOW THE MOVEMENT IS DONE:

With this hand movement we have our hands facing palm down, then we flip both hands over at the same time, so the palms are facing up; then you flip your hands, so the palms are facing down; continue flipping for as many repetitions as you like.

This Handy Brain movement helps use both sides of the brain at the same time, achieving some of the benefits listed on page 29.

HANDY BRAIN MOVEMENTS – FLIP HANDS

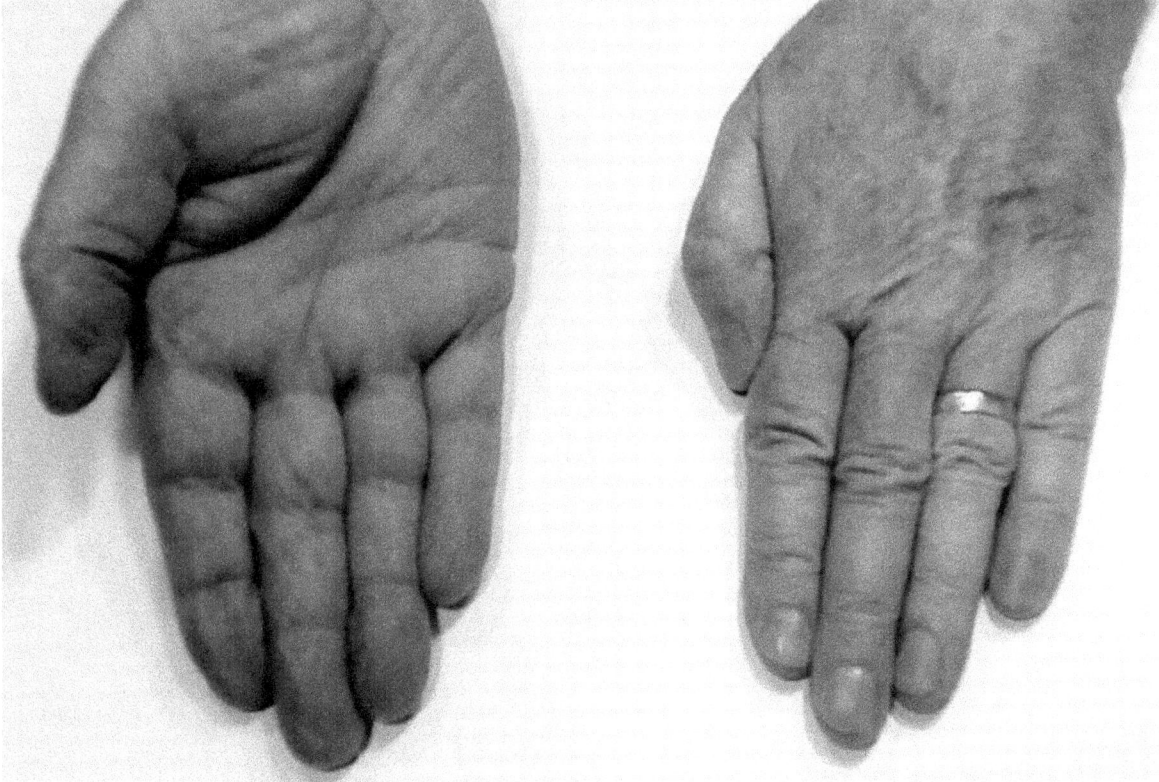

HOW THE MOVEMENT IS DONE:

With this hand movement we have the right-hand facing palm up, and the left hand facing palm down, then we flip our hands over at the same time, so the right-hand is now palm down and the left-hand is palm up; then we alternate both hands at the same time so one is palm up and the other is palm down.

This Handy Brain movement helps use both sides of the brain at the same time, achieving some of the benefits listed on page 29.

HANDY BRAIN MOVEMENTS – ONE IN - ONE OUT

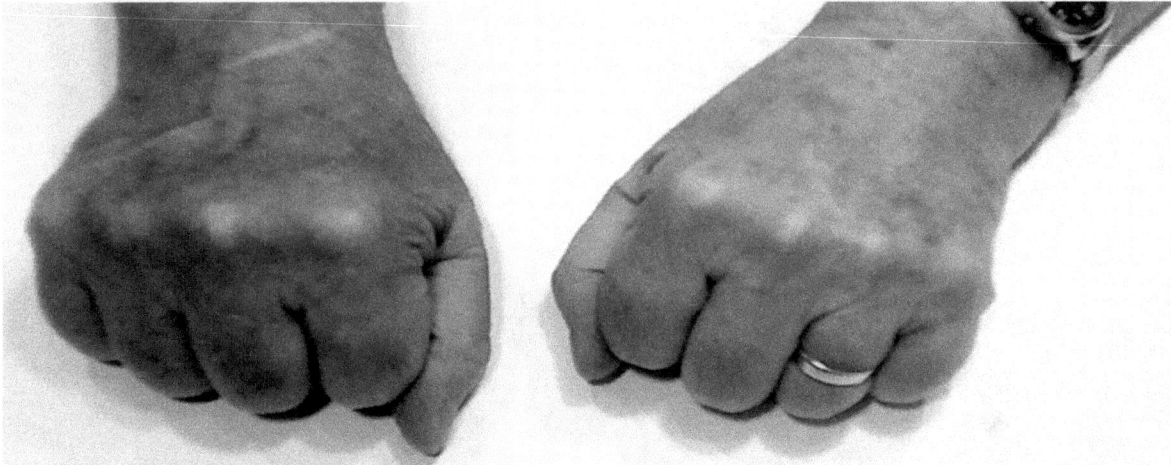

Right hand fingers out – left hand fingers in.

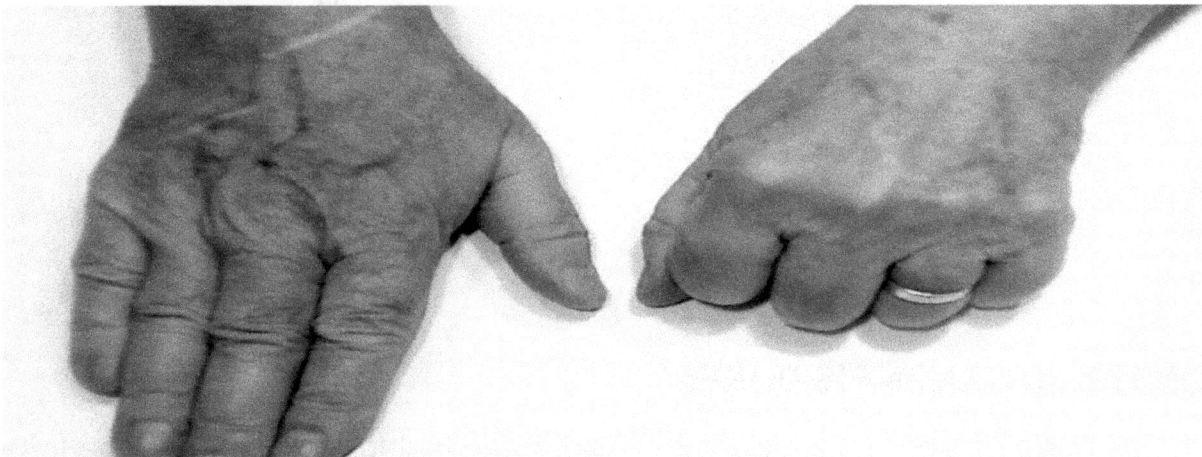

HOW THE MOVEMENT IS DONE:

Both hands are facing palm down in a clenched fist.

Then we move our right-hand fingers out and the left-hand as a clenched fist.

Then we switch the right-hand fingers into a clenched fist and the left-hand clenched fist to fingers out; we alternate both hands together as fingers out and clenched fist.

This Handy Brain movement helps use both sides of the brain at the same time, achieving some of the benefits listed on page 29.

HANDY BRAIN MOVEMENTS – THUMB IN – THUMB OUT

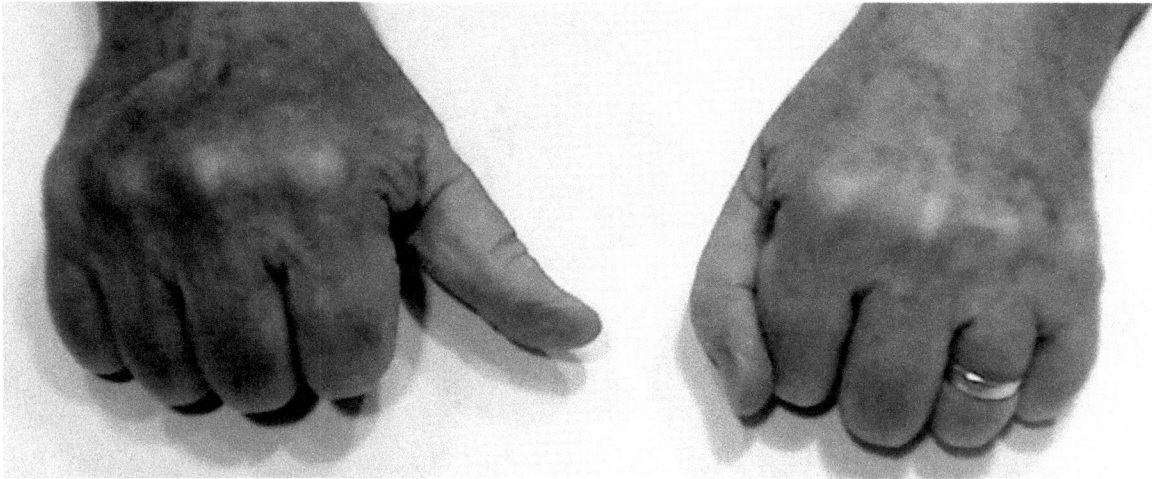

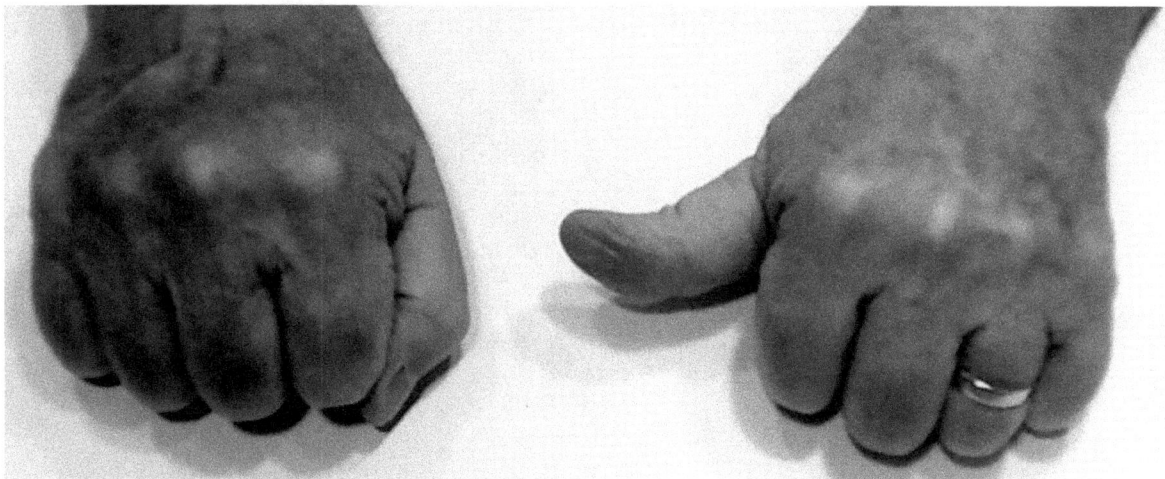

HOW THE MOVEMENT IS DONE:

Both hands are facing palm down in a clenched fist.

We have the right-hand with the thumb pointing out.

Then we move the right-hand thumb in and the left-hand moves the thumb out; we then alternate left-hand thumb in and the right-hand thumb out.

This Handy Brain movement helps use both sides of the brain at the same time, achieving some of the benefits listed on page 29.

THUMB OUT – LITTLE FINGER OUT

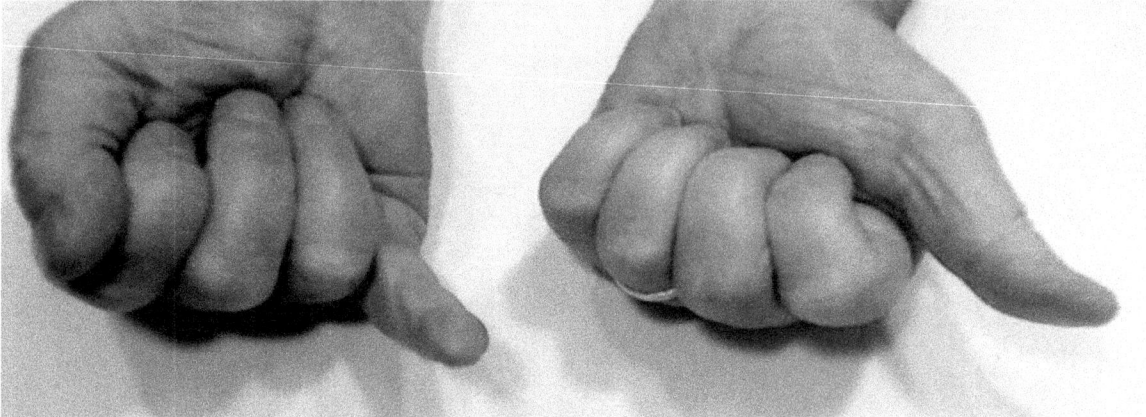

Change hands, little finger out thumb out.

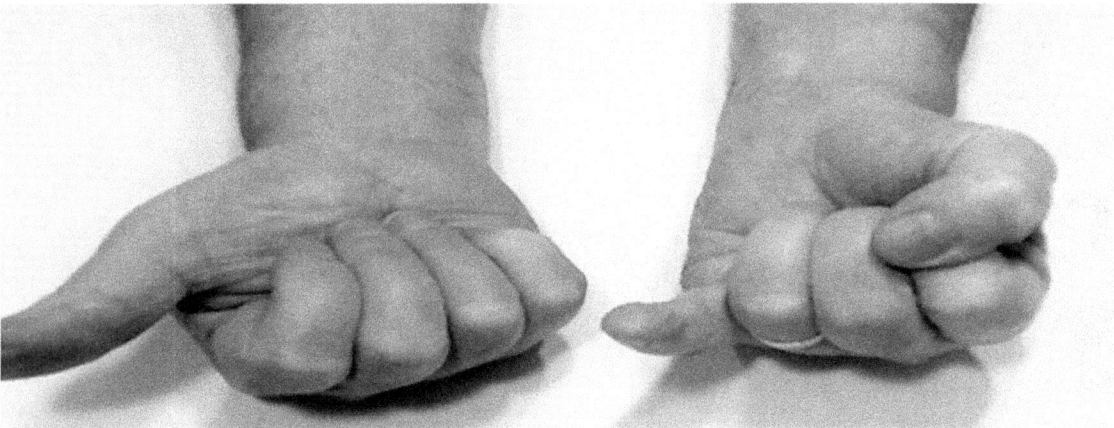

HOW THE MOVEMENT IS DONE:

Both hands are facing palm up with the left-hand thumb facing out and the right-hand little finger facing out.

Then we move the left-hand thumb in and the left-hand little finger out; at the same time, we move the right-hand little finger in and the right-hand thumb out.

Then we alternate between left-hand thumb out and the right-hand little finger out, switching to the left-hand little finger out and right-hand thumb out.

This Handy Brain movement helps use both sides of the brain at the same time, achieving some of the benefits listed on page 29.

SAME FINGERS OUT BOTH HANDS

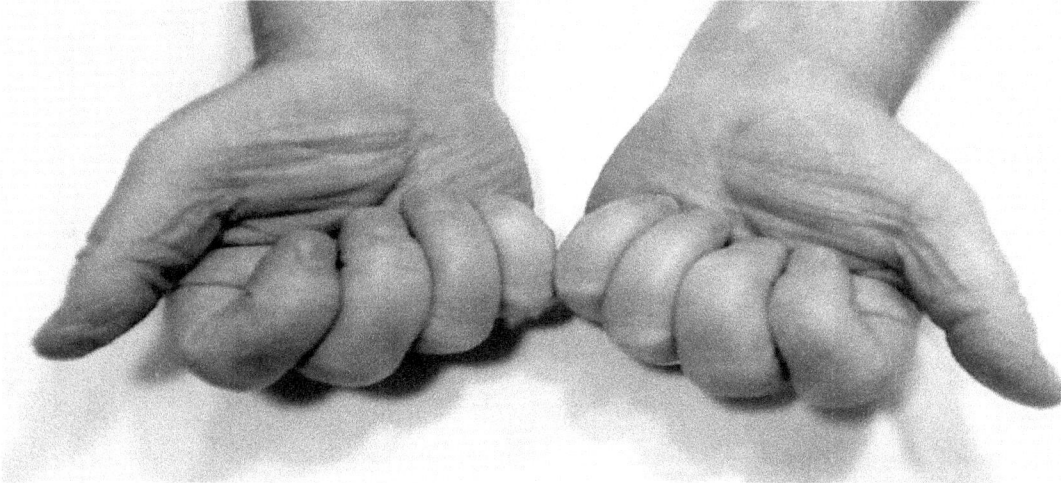

We put left- and right-hand same fingers out at the same time.

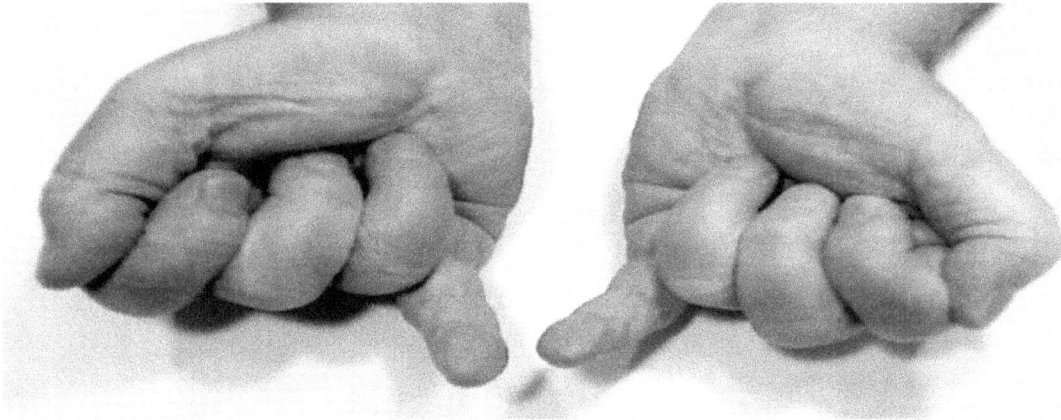

HOW THE MOVEMENT IS DONE:

Both hands are facing palm up in a clenched fist.

We move the left-hand and right-hand thumb out at the same time.

Then we move the thumbs in and move the little fingers out on both hands at the same time; we move the little fingers in and the next finger out; we move the same fingers on both hands in and out at the same time for each finger.

This Handy Brain movement helps use both sides of the brain at the same time, achieving some of the benefits listed on page 29.

INTERLINKED FINGERS

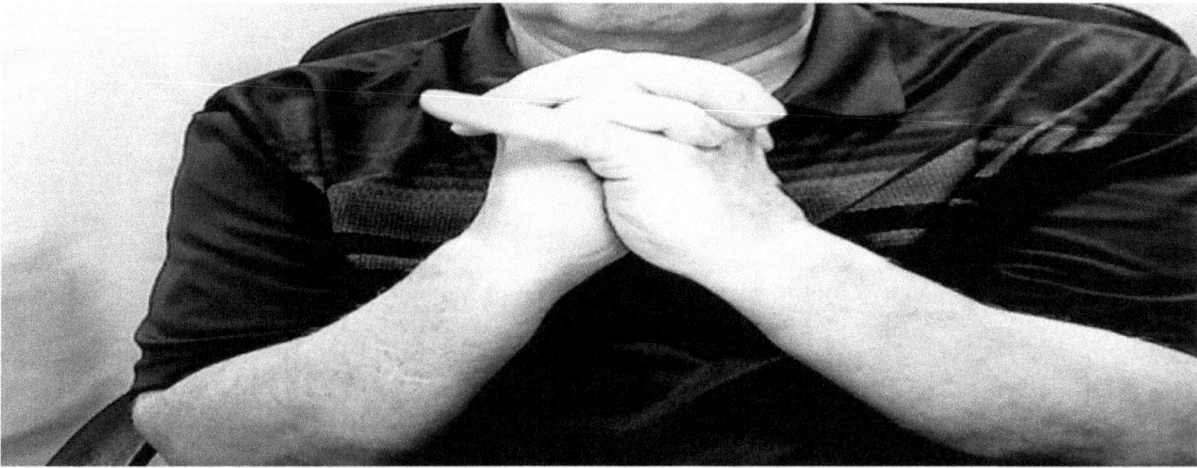

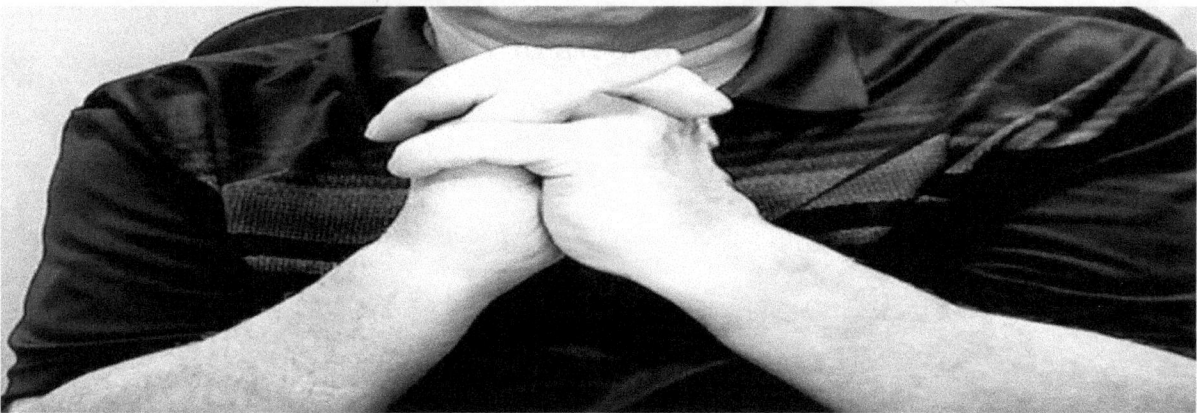

HOW THE MOVEMENT IS DONE:

We interlock the fingers of both hands.

We move the first left-hand little finger out.

Then we move the first left-hand little finger in and the finger next to it out, which is the right-hand little finger.

We then move the right-hand little finger in and the finger next to it out.

We start with the little finger on the left hand by moving it out and in, then we do the same for the finger next to it, until we do all the fingers moving in and out.

This Handy Brain movement helps use both sides of the brain at the same time, achieving some of the benefits listed on page 29.

Stopping smoking was one of the hardest things I have ever had to do in life; I enjoyed smoking, but I was using smoking to manage stress.

When I learned to meditate, I was using meditation to manage stress, so had less need to smoke cigarettes.

The incentive to stop smoking was how old I felt, at 27 I felt like I was 50 years old.

So, **"What is the secret to stopping smoking?"** In my case, I never stopped smoking, I just kept cutting down, until I was smoking no cigarettes a day.
Every time I wanted to smoke a cigarette, I made myself wait 5 minutes before I lit up the cigarette; I then increased the amount of time I waited to smoke the cigarette; over time waiting minutes turned into hours, then days.

Meditation helped with managing stress and a mindset of: "If I wanted to smoke, then I would" but I would wait the amount of time to smoke; then I was in control.
So, I never really stopped smoking, I just kept cutting down and increasing the amount of time between smokes; it has been 45 years since my last smoke.

How did I stop drinking, which was a bit easier, and was the day I nearly blinded my supervisor in a workplace accident.

I had been drinking on a lunchtime break; and was helping my supervisor fix a high-pressure autoclave that melted wax from ceramic molds; I brushed up against a relief valve that opened a valve which shot hot wax to where my supervisor was kneeling to fix the machine.

Fortunately for him, and me, the wax missed his eyes and landed on his hair; he had to cut off some of his hair to get rid of the wax, but otherwise he was unharmed.

That was the day I stopped drinking! When I was growing up, I was around uncles who were alcoholics; at 8 years old I told myself, "I will never be like them and cause any kind of harm to other people through drinking", yet here I was nearly blinding someone due my not being alert and under the influence of alcohol.

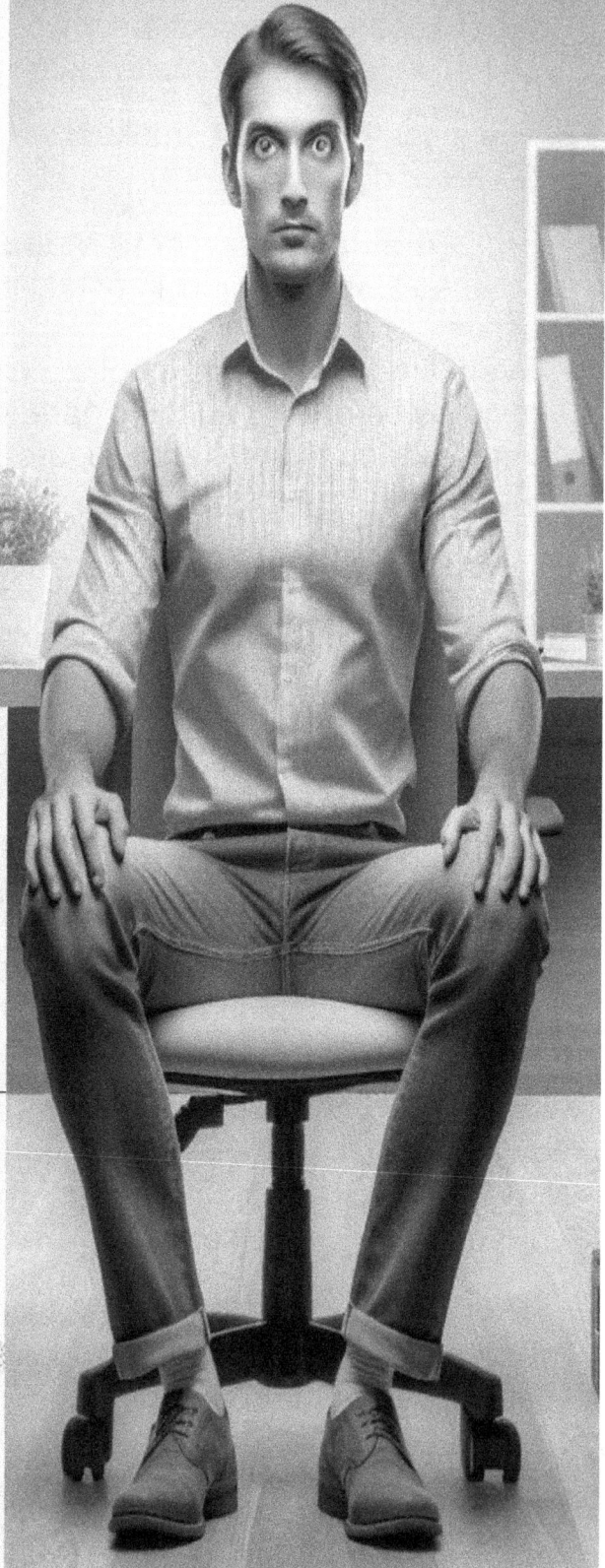

MEDITATION

When you think of meditation, do you see yourself sitting cross legged with your eyes closed?

That could be true of meditation, but it is not required; let us look at what meditation is and what the benefits are from meditation.

Meditation is conscious relaxation, a deeper form of concentration and generally results in clearing of the mind from distractions and helps with stress reduction.

Meditation can be:
- Calming.
- A form of conscious relaxation.
- A deeper form of concentration.
- Aa way that allows you to be in or leave the moment.

   Possible benefits:
- Reduction of anxiety.
- Preventing stress build up.
- Increased energy and productivity.
- Improved concentration and memory.
- Reduction of insomnia and fatigue.
- Increased self-confidence.

For a relaxing meditation, you need a:

1. Quiet place to relax.

2. A comfortable place to sit.

3. A sound, word, or something to focus on.

HERE ARE 5 WAYS TO MEDITATE:

MANTRA MEDITATION

This meditation technique should help you feel relaxed, energized, and focused.
Over time, the technique will become as natural as breathing, and will eventually require no effort or thought.

AN EASY AND EFFORTLESS WAY TO MEDITATE

1. Sit quietly in a comfortable position.

2. Close your eyes.

3. Let your body relax.

Notice your breathing, breath in through your nose (your stomach should rise), as you breathe out through your mouth (your stomach should fall), say the word, "ONE" silently, repeat the process: breathe in, breathe out, silently say "ONE;" breathe easily and naturally.

During the meditation, you will have thoughts.
When you realize you are thinking about something, return to the focus of breathing and silently say "ONE" as you exhale.

The average meditation time is 10 to 20 minutes.
You can check the time by opening your eyes, an alarm is not recommended; sit quietly for a few minutes before you finish.

The idea is to achieve a deep level of relaxation.
Do not worry whether your breathing is correct, or that you may have lots of thoughts, just simply return to the meditation technique.

Over time your breathing and technique will naturally occur.

GUIDED MEDITATION

Guided meditation is a form of meditation where an instructor or recorded voice leads participants through a series of visualizations, affirmations, or relaxation techniques. It typically involves closing the eyes, focusing on the breath, and following verbal cues to cultivate a state of deep relaxation and inner awareness. Here is a breakdown of the process and some benefits:

Participants find a comfortable seated or lying position, close their eyes, and begin to focus on their breath, gradually letting go of external distractions.
The instructor or recorded voice provides verbal instructions, such as directing attention to different parts of the body, visualizing calming scenes, or repeating affirmations.

POSSIBLE BENEFITS:
- Stress Reduction.
- Improved Focus.
- Emotional Regulation.
- Better Sleep.
- Enhanced Self-Awareness.
- Pain Management:

New meditators usually find it difficult to stay focused on one thought or sound, music helps provide the focus to help people concentrate.

The type of music does not have to be chants or classical, but some type of music that will help clear and re-direct the mind; it has been my experience to use music without words and mainly instrumental.

Select some calming instrumental music and find a comfortable, distraction-free space.
Close your eyes and focus on the music and your breathing.
Relax deeply and let the music guide your inner exploration.
Gradually transition back to awareness of your surroundings.

POSSIBLE BENEFITS:
- Stress Reduction.
- Enhanced Mood.
- Improved Focus.
- Relaxation.
- Mindfulness
- Emotional Release.
- Physical Relaxation
- Spiritual Connection

Standing meditation involves assuming a relaxed standing position while focusing on the breath or a specific point of awareness. It can be practiced with eyes open or closed, and the focus is on cultivating mindfulness and relaxation while standing still.

POSSIBLE BENEFITS:
- Improves posture and balance.
- Enhances body awareness.
- Promotes relaxation and stress reduction.
- Increases mental clarity and focus.
- Strengthens leg muscles and promotes circulation.
- Can be practiced anywhere, without the need for equipment.
- Cultivates mindfulness in daily activities.
- Enhances energy flow and vitality.
- Improves overall physical and mental well-being.

WALKING MEDITATION

Walking is an action meditation; the action of walking becomes your focus.

Walking meditations are always done with eyes open, but your awareness is on the environment, such as the sidewalk, people in the community, the rain, sun, wind; the things outside of yourself.

Walking meditations are usually best experienced in open spaces like forests, parks, open fields and generally allow you to walk unhindered for about 20 minutes.

TYPICAL WALKING MEDITATION
- Choose an open space.
- Walk at a slow, but normal pace.
- Be aware of your body.
- Be aware of how you are walking.
- Focus on and listen to external noises.

Personally, I have found Mantra Meditation to work best, as it can be done anywhere; and a simple sound mantra can help manage the number of excessive thoughts you may have in your head; over time.

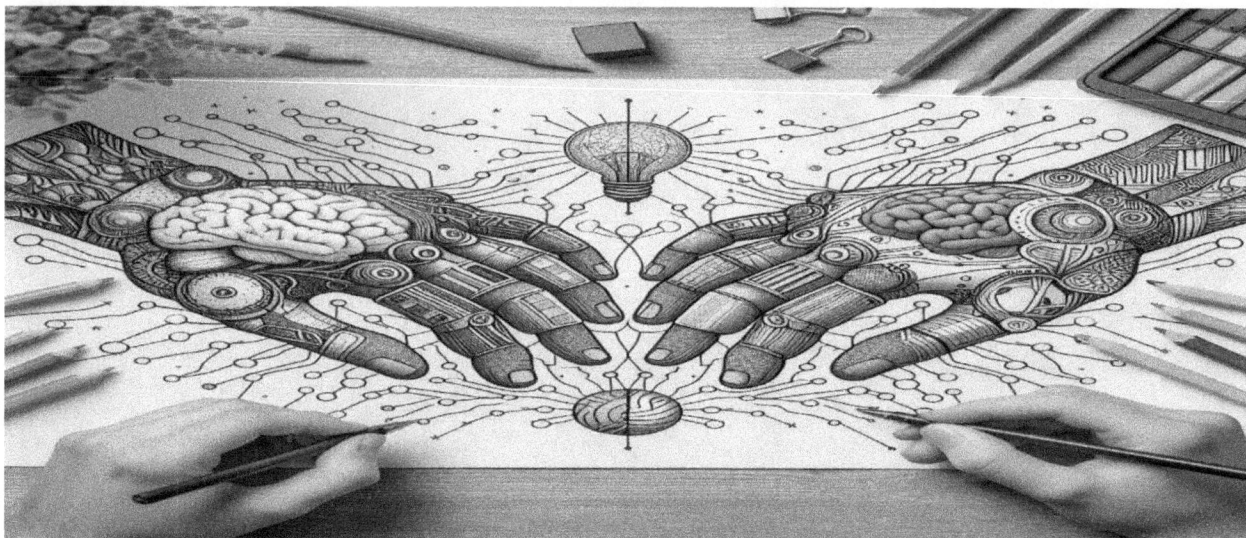

Coloring has many benefits, such as reducing stress; helps with concentration; self-expression; calms and relaxes; helps with grip and use of hands; hand eye coordination; and other benefits.

There are adult coloring books available from bookstores and online; with many topics to choose from.

If you are copying the coloring pages from this book, then it is best to print on heavy thicker paper and use coloring pencils. You can color using felt tips, watercolor paints, or other mediums, but you may get bleed through to the surface below the coloring page.

Adult coloring is not a childish activity and has been shown to have many therapeutic benefits.

Keep in mind: you do not have to color within the lines; just have fun and enjoy the activity; color any way you want to.

POSSIBLE BENEFITS:
- Stress reduction and relaxation.
- Increased focus and mindfulness.
- Enhanced creativity and self-expression.
- Improvement in fine motor skills and hand-eye coordination.
- Promotion of emotional well-being and mood regulation.
- Reduction in anxiety and symptoms of depression.
- Engagement in a calming and meditative activity.
- Distraction from negative thoughts and rumination.
- Encouragement of mindfulness and present moment awareness.
- Opportunity for self-care and personal reflection.

VISUALIZATION AND GETTING WHAT YOU WANT

Visualization is a technique where you mentally create vivid images or scenarios in your mind. It involves imagining specific details, sensations, and emotions associated with your desired outcome or goal. This practice can help enhance motivation, reduce stress, and improve performance.

HOW TO VISUALIZE:

- Find a quiet and comfortable space where you can relax.

- Close your eyes and take a few deep breaths to calm your mind.

- Visualize your desired outcome or goal in clear detail.

- Imagine yourself achieving success, experiencing every aspect of the situation as if it were real.

- Focus on specific details, such as colors, shapes, sounds, and emotions associated with your visualization.

- Stay positive and confident throughout the process, believing in your ability to manifest your goals.

- Practice visualization regularly, ideally incorporating it into your daily routine for maximum effectiveness.

NO MATTER HOW YOU FEEL
GET UP - DRESS UP - SHOW UP
AND NEVER GIVE UP

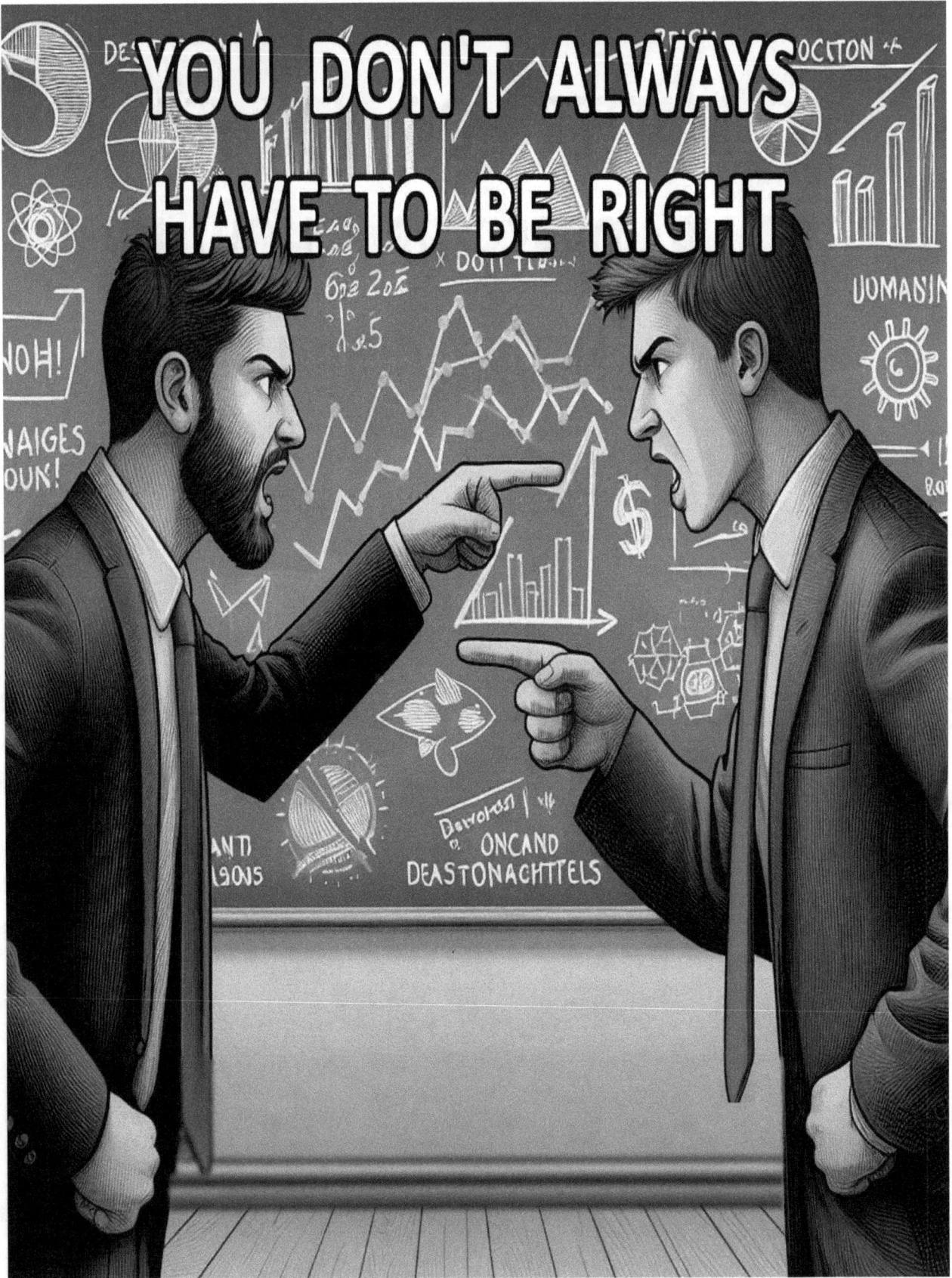

WORKPLACE STRESS MANAGEMENT COURSE

The purpose of this book is to:

- Help reduce stress in the workplace.
- Motivate and inspire the reader to achieve goals in life.
- Help the reader get through the workday in a balanced and harmonious way.

To achieve that purpose, I offer an online "Workplace Stress Management" course to groups or businesses.

The introductory webinar to the stress management course can be seen here:

https://www.workplacestressmanagement.com/webinar

The "Workplace Stress Management" Course Training will show you: basic movements and activities that could reduce stress, focus the mind, increase brain potential, motivate, energize, and get you through your day.

For more information contact Paul:

paulmackie@stressfreepreschool.com

ABOUT THE AUTHOR

Paul has had several careers, with certification as a Marine Engineer: Industrial Millwright, Welder, and Early Childhood Educator.

Paul has had experience as a Teacher's Assistant; Special Needs Childcare Worker; Brain Gym Instructor; Senior Building Manager.

Paul has taken courses of study such as "The writing Road to Reading," "Accelerated Learning" and other Brain development courses.

Paul has worked as a Community Care worker with special needs children, adults, and seniors; and has worked with children in Daycares, Day Programs, and the School System.

Paul is now retired; his last working position was as Senior Building Manager for a non-profit housing society.

Website Visit: https://www.workplacestressmanagement.com

Please feel free to leave a book review on Amazon or
Contact me at: paulmackie@stressfreepreschool.com

Have a great day.

Paul Mackie